You A
Takin

Publishing Information

Author: Travis Chapman

Publication Date: January 16, 2025

Edition: First Edition
Copyright: © [2025] by [Travis Chapman].

All rights reserved. No part of this book may be reproduced, stored in a retrieval system, or transmitted in any form or by any means, electronic, mechanical, photocopying, recording, or otherwise, without prior written permission from the publisher.

Printed in [US]

Table of Contents

1. Foreword
2. Introduction
3. Chapter 1: Control + Alt + Delete – The Power of Reset
4. Chapter 2: Escape – Finding Freedom
5. Chapter 3: Enter – Stepping Into Opportunities
6. Chapter 4: Backspace – Correcting Mistakes
7. Chapter 5: Shift – Changing Perspectives
8. Chapter 6: Tab – Exploring New Horizons
9. Chapter 7: Caps Lock – Amplifying Your Impact
10. Chapter 8: Ctrl + Z – Forgiving and Undoing
11. Chapter 9: Space Bar – Pausing and Breathing
12. Chapter 10: Delete – Letting Go
13. Conclusion

You Are The Human Keyboard: Taking Command of Your Life

Foreword

In a world where technology and humanity increasingly intersect, finding metaphors that bridge these realms is both timely and necessary. The keyboard, a tool we often take for granted, has become an integral part of our daily lives. It is the conduit through which we communicate, create, and solve problems. But beyond its practical use, the keyboard offers a profound metaphor for life itself—a guide to navigating its complexities, seizing its opportunities, and learning from its challenges.

When I first encountered the idea of using keyboard commands as a framework for personal growth, I was struck by its simplicity and depth. The commands we use every day—Control + Alt + Delete, Escape, Enter, Backspace—mirror the decisions and adjustments we make in our lives. Each keystroke carries meaning, each action a ripple effect. The more I thought about it, the more I realized how these lessons are embedded in the seemingly mundane tools we use to navigate the digital world.

This book is not just a manual for self-improvement; it's an invitation to see the world differently. It challenges us to rethink the way we approach setbacks, opportunities, and even the act of pausing to reflect. By examining the keyboard's commands through the lens of real-life scenarios and actionable processes, the author provides a practical and inspiring roadmap for personal transformation. Whether it's learning to reset your life with Control + Alt + Delete, shifting your perspective with Shift, or letting go of what no longer serves you with Delete, each chapter offers valuable insights for navigating life's complexities with intention and grace.

What I find most compelling about this book is its accessibility. The metaphor of the keyboard resonates with anyone who has ever typed a message, written a report, or surfed the internet. It breaks down the barriers between the abstract and the practical, making profound lessons feel within reach. The stories shared in these pages are relatable, the advice actionable, and the wisdom timeless.

As you embark on this journey, I encourage you to approach each chapter with an open mind and a willingness to reflect. This book is not about perfection but about progress. It's about understanding that life, like typing on a keyboard, is a series of small, deliberate actions that together create something meaningful. It's about realizing that every mistake is an opportunity to backspace, every challenge an invitation to press Enter, and every pause a chance to breathe and find clarity.

To the reader holding this book: consider it a map, a guide, a companion for the road ahead. As you explore the lessons within, may you discover the courage to take control, the wisdom to shift when needed, and the strength to let go of what no longer serves you. The keyboard may be a simple tool, but the life lessons it offers are profound. Now it's your turn to take the keys into your hands and start typing your story.

Introduction

Life often feels like a complex system, much like a computer, filled with challenges, opportunities, and unexpected errors. Each keystroke, each command, has the potential to change everything. Our choices, much like pressing a key, have a ripple effect on our paths, opening doors, closing others, and sometimes requiring us to reboot entirely. A keyboard, in its simplicity, holds profound lessons for living with intention and clarity.

The keyboard is one of the most universal tools, accessible to nearly everyone in the modern world. We use it daily to communicate, create, and solve problems. Yet, its potential as a metaphor for life often goes unnoticed. Think of the Control + Alt + Delete command that provides a system reset or the Tab key that helps us move seamlessly from one field to the next. These commands mirror the choices, shifts, and adjustments we make in our daily lives to adapt and thrive.

At its core, the keyboard is a map of human behavior—a guide to navigating challenges, opportunities, and moments of reflection. Just as we use the keyboard to interface with technology, we can use its lessons to interface with life's complexities. Each key offers a different pathway, from pressing Escape to exit toxic situations, to hitting Enter to commit to bold new opportunities, to Backspace to correct mistakes and learn from them.

This book is about uncovering the wisdom hidden within these commands and applying it to your life. Just as a skilled typist masters the keyboard to increase efficiency and creativity, mastering the metaphors of the keyboard can empower you to live with intention, resilience, and clarity. By aligning your actions with the lessons these commands provide, you can unlock a deeper understanding of yourself and the world around you.

Consider the keyboard's layout—each key has a specific purpose, yet they work in harmony. Life operates the same way. Each decision, no matter how small, contributes to the greater picture. Like a well-crafted sentence formed by carefully chosen keys, a meaningful life is built on deliberate choices and purposeful actions. This perspective allows us to embrace the messiness of life with curiosity and determination.

As you read this book, you'll explore the power of each key, discovering how its function on a keyboard translates into life's challenges and opportunities. From letting go of what no longer serves you with the Delete key to amplifying your presence with Caps Lock, each chapter will guide you through real-life scenarios, practical processes, and actionable advice. These stories and insights are designed to inspire you to take control of your journey and press the keys that align with your goals.

Ultimately, this book is about empowerment. The keyboard's commands are not just tools for computers—they are metaphors for how to live a life of abundance, growth, and authenticity. Whether you need to pause and breathe by pressing Space, undo a mistake with Ctrl + Z, or shift your perspective to see things anew, the lessons of the keyboard are here to guide you. Life is a series of keystrokes, each one building on the last to create a meaningful story.

So, sit down at your metaphorical keyboard. Place your fingers on the keys of life. And let's start typing a new chapter together.

Chapter 1: Control + Alt + Delete – The Power of Reset

When your computer becomes unresponsive or overwhelmed, pressing **Control + Alt + Delete** provides a way to restart or end processes that no longer serve you. Similarly, in life, we sometimes encounter moments where we feel stuck, overwhelmed, or bogged down by outdated habits or toxic relationships.

Real-Life Scenarios:

Jessica's Reset Jessica was a marketing executive juggling long hours and personal commitments. When her health started to decline, she realized she needed to hit reset. Jessica identified her stressors, explored alternatives like delegating tasks, and let go of unnecessary obligations. This reset allowed her to regain control of her health and work-life balance.

Mike's Career Change Mike had spent 15 years in the same job, feeling unchallenged and uninspired. His wake-up call came when he realized he dreaded Monday mornings. By pressing Control + Alt + Delete in his career, Mike took time to assess his skills and passions. He attended networking events, updated his resume, and enrolled in a certification program. Within a year, he transitioned into a role that reignited his passion.

Family Dynamics Reset Karen and her teenage daughter found themselves constantly arguing, leading to tension in their home. Karen decided to apply the Control + Alt + Delete philosophy to their relationship. She set aside time to listen to her daughter's concerns, explored alternative ways of communication like family counseling, and let go of her need to micromanage. This reset brought harmony back into their household.

The Process:

1. **Control:** Identify areas of your life where you have influence. Take inventory of your priorities.
    - Create a list of what you can and cannot control.
    - Focus on what aligns with your goals.

2. **Alt:** Explore alternative strategies to handle your challenges. Consider delegating or simplifying your commitments.
    - Look for new opportunities that resonate with your values.
    - Experiment with different approaches to problem-solving.

3. **Delete:** Eliminate what drains your energy. Whether

it's toxic relationships or unproductive habits, let them go.

- Start small by removing one toxic element at a time.
- Embrace minimalism to simplify your lifestyle.

Resetting isn't failure; it's an intentional step toward clarity and renewal.

Chapter 2: Escape – Finding Freedom

The **Escape** key is a lifesaver when you need to exit a program or undo an unwanted action. In life, the Escape key reminds us that we always have the power to walk away from situations that don't align with our values or well-being.

Real-Life Scenarios:

David's Career Shift David found himself in a job that paid well but drained his spirit. After months of feeling trapped, he decided to press Escape. He planned his exit strategy, enrolled in night classes to pursue his passion for teaching, and eventually transitioned to a fulfilling career.

Sarah's Boundary Setting Sarah had been in a long-term friendship that felt one-sided and emotionally draining. By pressing Escape, she set boundaries, prioritized self-care, and eventually phased out the relationship. This created space for healthier connections.

An Escape from Burnout Tom was a small business owner who worked 80-hour weeks, leaving little time for his family or hobbies. Recognizing the toll on his health, he decided to press Escape by hiring additional staff and delegating responsibilities. This allowed him to rediscover his love for painting and spend more time with his children.

The Process:

1. **Recognize:** Acknowledge the situations that no longer serve you.
    - Journal your feelings to identify sources of unhappiness.
2. **Plan:** Develop an exit strategy that includes realistic steps and timelines.

- Seek advice from mentors or trusted friends.

3. **Act:** Take action to leave the toxic environment, even if it's one small step at a time.
    - Celebrate each milestone in your journey toward freedom.

Escaping isn't about quitting; it's about prioritizing your happiness and growth.

Chapter 3: Enter – Stepping Into Opportunities

The **Enter** key is about taking action and moving forward. It symbolizes commitment and the courage to say "Yes" to new opportunities.

Real-Life Scenarios:

Maria's Bakery Dream Maria had always wanted to start her own bakery but hesitated due to fear of failure. One day, she decided to press Enter. She took a small step by selling her goods at a local farmers' market. As her confidence grew, so did her business, eventually becoming a successful bakery.

Jake's Fitness Journey Jake struggled with his health for years but decided to press Enter when his doctor warned him about potential complications. He committed to a simple daily walk, gradually building up to a full fitness routine. Over time, he lost weight and gained a new lease on life.

Sophia's Public Speaking Breakthrough Sophia avoided public speaking at all costs, fearing embarrassment. When her boss asked her to present at a company meeting, she decided to press Enter. She prepared diligently, practiced with friends, and delivered a successful presentation. This led to more opportunities to showcase her leadership.

The Process:

1. **Identify:** Recognize opportunities that align with your passions and goals.
    - Write down your dreams and break them into actionable steps.

2. **Commit:** Take small but decisive steps to move toward your dream.
    - Say "Yes" to opportunities, even if they feel daunting.

3. **Persevere:** Embrace challenges as part of the journey and keep moving forward.
    - Reflect on progress and adjust your approach as needed.

Pressing Enter opens the door to growth and transformation.

Chapter 4: Backspace – Correcting Mistakes

The **Backspace** key allows you to erase errors and try again. In life, we all make mistakes, but the ability to acknowledge them and make corrections is a powerful skill.

Real-Life Scenarios:

Ethan's Business Mistake After a failed business venture, Ethan felt defeated. Instead of giving up, he reflected on what went wrong and made adjustments. With a revised plan, he launched a new venture that thrived, thanks to lessons learned from his mistakes.

Rachel's Parenting Do-Over Rachel had a heated argument with her teenage son and regretted the harsh words she used. She pressed Backspace by apologizing and opening a dialogue with him. This strengthened their relationship and improved their communication.

Michael's Academic Comeback

Michael failed a critical college exam and felt like giving up. Instead, he reviewed his study habits, sought help from a tutor, and practiced diligently. By pressing Backspace on his initial failures, he aced the next exam and restored his confidence.

The Process:

1. **Acknowledge:** Accept your mistakes without self-judgment.
2. **Learn:** Reflect on what went wrong and identify lessons.
3. **Adjust:** Implement changes and try again with newfound wisdom.

Mistakes are not failures; they are opportunities for growth.

Chapter 5: Shift – Changing Perspectives

The **Shift** key transforms lowercase letters to uppercase, signaling a change or elevation. In life, pressing Shift represents the power to change your perspective and elevate your thinking.

Real-Life Scenarios:

Emily's Mindset Shift Emily had always viewed challenges as obstacles. After attending a seminar on resilience, she shifted her perspective and began seeing them as opportunities for growth. This mindset change enabled her to tackle problems with optimism and creativity, leading to professional and personal breakthroughs.

Brian's Relationship Shift Brian and his partner were on the verge of separation due to constant disagreements. By shifting his focus from being "right" to understanding his partner's needs, Brian transformed their communication. This shift saved their relationship and deepened their connection.

The Process:

1. **Recognize:** Identify areas where your perspective may be limiting growth.
    - Journal situations where you feel stuck or negative.

2. **Reframe:** Shift your focus to a more empowering perspective.
    - Replace thoughts like "I failed" with "I learned something valuable."

3. **Act:** Take intentional steps to embody your new perspective.
    - Engage in activities or conversations that reinforce the shift.

A small shift in thinking can lead to significant changes in outcomes.

Chapter 6: Tab – Exploring New Horizons

The **Tab** key allows us to move between fields or tasks efficiently. In life, pressing Tab represents the importance of exploring new horizons and transitioning smoothly between opportunities.

Real-Life Scenarios:

Anna's Career Exploration Anna was unsure about her career path but decided to press Tab by attending workshops and networking events in different industries. This exploration led her to discover a passion for digital marketing, where she found both success and fulfillment.

Mark's Social Circles Mark felt stuck in his social life and decided to tab through different groups by joining local meetups and volunteering. This exploration expanded his circle and introduced him to lifelong friendships.

The Process:

1. **Explore:** Identify areas where you'd like to broaden your horizons.
    - List hobbies, careers, or communities you've been curious about.
2. **Engage:** Take the first step to learn or participate.
    - Attend a class, read a book, or talk to someone in that field.
3. **Evaluate:** Reflect on your experiences and adjust accordingly.
    - Decide whether to dive deeper or explore another avenue.

Exploring new horizons keeps life dynamic and full of potential.

Chapter 7: Caps Lock – Amplifying Your Impact

The **Caps Lock** key emphasizes text, drawing attention to important elements. In life, pressing Caps Lock is about amplifying your voice, actions, and passions to create a lasting impact.

Real-Life Scenarios:

Tina's Advocacy Work Tina was passionate about animal welfare but felt her efforts were insignificant. By pressing Caps Lock, she started an online campaign, organized fundraisers, and connected with local shelters. Her amplified actions raised awareness and funds, creating meaningful change.

James's Career Visibility James wanted to be recognized as a leader in his field. By writing articles, speaking at events, and mentoring others, he amplified his expertise. This visibility opened doors to promotions and opportunities to influence his industry.

The Process:

1. **Identify:** Choose an area where you want to amplify your efforts.
   - Focus on passions or strengths you're proud of.
2. **Strategize:** Develop a plan to share your message or actions.
   - Use social media, community events, or personal networks.
3. **Execute:** Take consistent, bold steps to amplify your presence.
   - Celebrate small wins to build momentum.

Amplifying your impact inspires others and drives meaningful change.

Chapter 8: Ctrl + Z – Forgiving and Undoing

The **Ctrl + Z** command undoes the last action, offering a chance to correct mistakes. In life, Ctrl + Z represents forgiveness and the ability to start fresh.

Real-Life Scenarios:

Lila's Self-Forgiveness After a failed business venture, Lila struggled with guilt and self-doubt. By pressing Ctrl + Z, she forgave herself, learned from her mistakes, and started a new venture with renewed confidence.

David's Reconciliation David had a falling-out with his best friend over a misunderstanding. He pressed Ctrl + Z by reaching out, apologizing, and expressing his desire to mend the relationship. Their friendship was restored and strengthened.

The Process:

1. **Acknowledge:** Reflect on the situation and its impact.
    - Identify what needs undoing or forgiving.
2. **Apologize:** If others are involved, offer a sincere apology.
    - Take responsibility without excuses.
3. **Release:** Let go of guilt, anger, or resentment.
    - Focus on moving forward with a clean slate.

Undoing doesn't erase the past but creates space for healing and growth.

Chapter 9: Space Bar – Pausing and Breathing

The **Space Bar** creates a pause, giving structure to words and sentences. In life, pressing Space represents the need to pause, reflect, and breathe.

Real-Life Scenarios:

Maya's Burnout Recovery Maya was overwhelmed by her job and personal responsibilities. By pressing Space, she scheduled daily pauses for meditation and weekly nature walks. These pauses improved her mental clarity and overall well-being.

Evan's Career Transition Evan felt trapped in a stressful job but was unsure about his next steps. He pressed Space by taking a sabbatical to reflect on his values and goals. This pause led him to a fulfilling new career.

The Process:

1. **Pause:** Set aside time to step away from daily demands.
    - Use techniques like mindfulness or journaling.
2. **Reflect:** Assess your current state and what needs attention.
    - Ask yourself questions about your goals and priorities.
3. **Recharge:** Engage in activities that restore your energy.
    - Prioritize rest, hobbies, and meaningful connections.

Pausing allows you to realign with your purpose and regain clarity.

Chapter 10: Delete – Letting Go

The **Delete** key removes unnecessary elements, clearing the way for improvement. In life, pressing Delete symbolizes the power of letting go of what no longer serves you.

Real-Life Scenarios:

Nina's Minimalist Journey Nina felt overwhelmed by physical clutter in her home. By pressing Delete, she embraced minimalism, letting go of items she no longer needed. This decluttering brought peace and simplicity to her life.

Jake's Toxic Relationship Jake realized his friendship with a coworker was draining his energy and confidence. He pressed Delete by setting boundaries and focusing on healthier connections.

The Process:

1. **Identify:** Pinpoint what no longer serves your well-being.
    - Reflect on habits, relationships, or commitments that drain you.
2. **Decide:** Make a conscious choice to let go.
    - Start small by addressing one area at a time.
3. **Act:** Remove these elements from your life.
    - Celebrate the space you create for new opportunities.

Letting go creates room for growth and renewal.

Conclusion

As we reach the end of this journey, let us reflect on the wisdom and simplicity of the keyboard. It is more than a tool for communication and productivity; it is a profound metaphor for navigating life. Each key, with its unique function, represents an aspect of the human experience—our ability to reset, adapt, take bold steps, correct mistakes, and let go.

Life, much like typing, is a sequence of deliberate actions. Each keystroke, whether it is a mistake corrected by Backspace or an opportunity embraced with Enter, contributes to the greater story we are writing. This book has shown that the lessons embedded in the keyboard's commands are not just practical; they are transformative. They remind us that we hold the power to navigate life's complexities with intention, grace, and resilience.

As you move forward, remember to:

- **Reset** when life feels overwhelming, using Control + Alt + Delete to start fresh.
- **Escape** situations that no longer serve your well-being.
- **Enter** opportunities with courage and commitment.
- **Backspace** to learn from and correct your mistakes.
- **Shift** your perspective to unlock new ways of thinking.
- **Tab** through life's possibilities to discover new horizons.
- **Caps Lock** your impact by amplifying your passions and strengths.
- **Ctrl + Z** to forgive and undo when necessary, allowing for healing.
- **Press Space** to pause, breathe, and reflect.

- **Delete** what no longer aligns with your goals to make room for growth.

Every key is a reminder that we are in control of the narrative we type each day. You are the author of your story, and the keyboard is your guide. Whether you are resetting after a challenge or stepping into a new chapter, know that the keys are always within reach, ready to support you.

So, go forth and type your life's story with intention, creativity, and confidence. The world is your document, and the possibilities are limitless. May you press the keys that align with your dreams and create a masterpiece uniquely your own.

Made in the USA
Columbia, SC
07 February 2025